GET THE
SKINNY

ON

MAKING MONEY
AT HOME

DUANE SHINN

GET THE SKINNY™ BOOKS

An Imprint of Morgan James Publishing

Garden City, New York • www.morganjamespublishing.com

GET THE SKINNY ON: MAKING MONEY AT HOME

ISBN: 1-933596-80-5 (Paperback)
ISBN: 1-60037-060-8 (eBook)
ISBN: 1-60037-061-6 (Audio)

Published by:

MORGAN · JAMES
THE ENTREPRENEURIAL PUBLISHER™
www.morganjamespublishing.com

Morgan James Publishing, LLC
1225 Franklin Ave Ste 325
Garden City, NY 11530-1693
Toll Free 800-485-4943
www.MorganJamesPublishing.com

Habitat
for Humanity®
Peninsula
Building Partner

Cover & Interior Design by:
3 Dog Design
www.3dogdesign.net
chris@3dogdesign.net

Acknowledgements

I would first like to acknowledge my awesome God to whom I owe not only all the joys of life but also my very existence. He brings meaning and excitement to every area of my life, and gives me far, far more than I deserve. Plus He forgives me when I blow it.

And of course I would like to thank my beautiful & elegant wife & lover Bev, who has stood along side me for lo these many years and helped build our home business using talents I do not have. And our four wonderful kids - Kurt, Kendra, Garin & Garth - all grown now - who spent many an evening in their pajamas helping Mom and Dad insert music books into manila envelopes - books that Dad had written and sold to catalog houses such as Miles Kimball, Sunset House and many others.

I would also like to thank the many people who contributed to this book in one way or another, including my great neighbor and inspiring friend Norm Bruce; my computer guys Mark Shelamer and Kevin Follett and Brad Pankonin; my CD and DVD guy Darryl Coulombe who also works at home; my friend and printer Arnie Klott; my go-to digital guy, Pat Pelzel; and a host of great friends who have home businesses of varying sizes including Craig Black, Shirley Buckmaster, Curt Morse, Dave & Laura Vaughn, my brother Garland and his wife Roberta and many others.

God bless you every one!

GET THE **SKINNY** ON:

Contents

Chapter ①

The Many Incredible Benefits of Working at Home & The 3 Hurdles That Must be Overcome

I've got lot of good news for you, but I've also got some bad news. So let's take the bad news first and get it out of the way.

There are 3 disadvantages of working at home:

1) *You don't get a gold watch when you retire. There are no retirement benefits coming except for social security, unless you create those benefits yourself.*

2) *You don't get insurance benefits. That's a HUGE disadvantage that absolutely must be overcome.*

3) *You don't get a paid vacation. You can take a vacation, but you have to pay for it.*

If these 3 drawbacks scare you to death – especially the lack of insurance benefits – good. These cannot be ignored, but they can be overcome, and everyone who works at home deals with them differently.

If you have a job now, stay on that job until you have enough income from your home business to buy private insurance. In my case, I was blessed with a wonderful wife who worked part-time at a local hospital 2 days a week for several years while our home business was getting off the ground. Without that insurance and with 4 kids, we would have been in big trouble. So if you have a job that has insurance benefits, stay where you are until you can either cut back your hours and still get insurance, or until you can afford to buy insurance on your own.

And by the way, you'll waste a lot of time searching for insurance on your own. Instead, look in your local phone book for an insurance broker, and when you find one you feel comfortable with, they will do all the searching for the best policies that fit your needs, and you won't pay any more for their services – they are paid by the insurance company.

Retirement benefits are a different matter. If you build a home business doing the things you love anyway, you won't be very interested in retirement. I have friends who have retired and then gotten bored with doing nothing, and have gone back to work. If you love what you do in the first place, you won't have that problem. And if you build that home business up to a very profitable point, you can sell it at some point and retire, if that's what you want to do.

Vacations are a little more iffy. Even though you don't get paid for taking time off from your work, you need to anyway – just to clear your mind and get perspective. Some of my very best ideas have come to me while I was taking a "break-ation", so instead of costing me, it actually was both beneficial and profitable. My suggestion would be this: when you're in the start-up phase of your home business, take long weekend breaks. If you take a Friday and a Monday off, you've got 4 days to travel or rest or just get away, and yet you haven't been away from your business for a week or more, as is common with most vacations. So take several "break-ations" throughout the year, taking advantage of long holiday weekends to maximize your vacation time.

Now that we have that out of the way, let's take a look at the 10 incredible benefits (and there are probably more) of your own home business:

1) No boss! (But you had better be your own good boss - if you want to get anything done.) If you don't have self-discipline and spend most of the morning watching the news on TV, then you have no business working at home. You need a boss to keep you accountable.

2) No commute! I can hear cheers from the Los Angeles freeway system. I well remember those LONG drives from the Azusa-Covina area into downtown LA when we were first married. No thanks!

3) No time clock! But again - you had better have self-discipline if you are going to work for yourself. If you put in 3 hours a day you'll soon find out that your paycheck will reflect that.

4) No child care! Time with the fam! One of the things I loved about working for myself at home was that I was always able to attend my kid's games, concerts, etc. That is a HUGE plus. I saw my kids go to school, and I saw them come home. That benefit alone is worth more than Bill Gates net worth!

5) No dressing up! Heck, no dressing period. If you want to work in your underwear, that's up to you. And sometimes in the middle of the night, I do.

6) The exhilarating sense of freedom creating your own product or service! Nothing is quite so satisfying as seeing your own ideas come to fruition in a book or a product or a service that you have envisioned and worked toward.

7) The joy of doing what you love, whatever that is for you. I love the piano and music and people, so it's hardly work to do what I would do anyway! I love to share what I have learned about music

and the piano, so getting paid to do what I would do for free is a
wonderful feeling.

8) No limits. You can build your home business into any size you
like - the world is your market. You can keep it small if you
like, or you can grow as big as you like - it's all up to you.
The Internet has made dealing with people in Hong Kong and
Singapore and Stockholm almost as easy as dealing with people
in your hometown.

9) You have time. Time to focus on cutting edge tools such as
blogs and podcasts and other exciting ways to make your home
business known to the world. New avenues of communication are
opening up every year, so by working for yourself you are not
limited by company restrictions. You can pursue any fields you find
interesting and exciting.

10) Tax benefits. I'm not an accountant by any means (and it will
pay you to find a good accountant right now, before you take the
home-business leap), but if you earn substantial income from your
home business, you can usually write off a portion of your phone
bill, your utility bill, and other expenses necessary for running your
home business.

The wonderful benefits of having your own home business far
outweigh any perceived disadvantages in my book.

Try it - I think you'll like it.

On second thought - I think you're gonna LOVE it as much as I do!

Chapter 2

Lots of Others Are Working At Home – How About You?

There has never been a better time in history than right now to start and develop your own business right at home. Just a few years ago there was no computer networking, so it was difficult to transfer the work you did at home to your place of business. But no more. With the development of the personal computer, people can work anywhere – and they are – in record numbers.

But in certain fields you can still do it, even if you don't know how to use a computer, or if you choose not to. Here are a few examples of real people working out of their homes in vastly different fields.

Baseball Pitching Machines

A neighbor of mine named Norm Bruce has worked at home for over 30 years – and without the benefit of a computer. A computer would have helped, but he managed just fine without one. It all began when he was a Little League coach and became frustrated because his young hitters were not progressing satisfactorily after three weeks. "So I designed a little machine to throw plastic balls," said Norm, modestly. "The season began slowly as our team hit .150. When the season ended, we were hitting .450. It was quickly apparent that we had something special with this machine because it took away the fear of being hit by pitches with real baseballs. The Granada

Pitching Machine was born. At the time Norm was working as a meter-reader in the Los Angeles area, but believed he could develop his pitching machine to the point where it would support he and his family. So he and his wife Betty & their two sons moved to Oregon and built his own house with a big shop and area where he could build his machines without leaving home. His two boys, Paul and John, helped him as much as they could.

One of the benefits of Norm's pitching machine was that kids were no longer afraid of being hit by a hard ball, so they loved to practice hitting and Norm was asked what the ideal number of daily swings are when using his machine from youth level on up.

"There is a general feeling that you should not extend 9 and 10 year-olds too much. When they are tired, simply stop. But when Paul got a little older, he hit 1,000 poly balls a day with our machine and broke those cuts into seven sessions a day. In each one of those sessions, he probably got more cuts than the average school player had in a month of regular practice. So if you break down the numbers, he got a half a year's practice for the typical player in one day."

"Paul said one summer he took over 100,000 cuts. It was not hard to believe he was a superb hitter in his playing days who made pitchers extremely nervous. In his playing career, which went into college, he estimates he took over a half million cuts because of his great passion for the game."

If you wonder how Paul picked up 1,000 balls a day without destroying his back, here is how he did it. Norm came up with a system where hit polyballs would stay in a cage Paul was in, roll in a certain direction after they hit the slightly slanted wooden floor and be picked up by cups along a belt system in a gutter which would deposit poly balls into the machine one at a time every 3-5 seconds, depending on how fast it was set.

Norm's polyball pitching machines have been endorsed by such coaching legends as Gordie Gillespie, the winningest 4-year college coach in history. "His poly ball machines have really helped baseball in numerous ways, especially for the northern baseball teams," said Gillespie. "Those of us in the cold weather areas have to practice indoors quite a bit, and his poly ball machines have been the greatest asset to us. I am a huge advocate of his machines. Being confined like we are indoors, we hardly ever hit a real baseball (during practice). His machines are very accurate. About 95 percent of the time balls go exactly where you want them to go. His machines are the greatest invention to get young children started in baseball. His poly balls take the fear factor out. You can have young kids 7, 8 and 9 years old get hit by a baseball, and they never come back. The poly ball machine keeps them in the game and helps them learn. It's the greatest teaching device.

Jerry Stitt, head baseball coach at the University of Arizona, has known Norm for many years and treasures his relationship with him and the rest of the Bruce family. "Those of us in the coaching profession who have known him for years and years have the greatest respect for him and what he has done for baseball on all levels," said Stitt.

"He is deeply committed and has passion for the game that is rare. He has been such an important person to the game of baseball. Norm is one of those special people who never asks anything from anybody. But he always gives so much. That is a wonderful quality which is special about him."

Norm was asked who some of the celebrities have been who have purchased his machines. He said they include NFL Coaches George Allen and Ted Marchibroda, and Major League greats Pete Rose,

George Brett and Tony Gwynn, to name a few. His machines are still widely used by teams from the Major League down to Little League.

And remember – all this was done working out of his home. The only times he had to be gone was when he traveled to baseball clinics to demonstrate his Granada pitching machines. The benefits of Norm working out of his own home have been beneficial not only for his family, but for the entire baseball world as well!

Norm has now passed the torch to Mark Shellamer who continues the tradition of marketing the Granada Pitching Machine out of his home. Check out his web site at www.battingpractice.com

Books Recorded Onto CD's & Tapes

Twenty years ago Craig Black was commuting three hours a day from his home into downtown Los Angeles in his job as an executive for a manufacturer. Some days he spent more time on the freeway than he did relaxing at home. It was work, sleep, work, sleep, and work all over again. He worked for Tenneco West, a division of Tenneco. They had hired him to start-up a mall store venture, to sell a brand that they had developed called House of Almonds. When he left, there were about 350 stores in malls all across the US. That's one reason he now loathes spending time in enclosed shopping malls, as well as driving that long miserable commute into Los Angeles.

To pass the time on his daily commute, he would often listen to books that had been recorded on cassette tape as he drove or was stalled in traffic jams. An idea gradually began to form in his mind about doing the same thing to some of the older classics that were out of copyright. One thing led to another, and in 1989 he made the move by quitting his job, moving to Oregon, and recording his first classic book on tape. His first title was Compassion Vs. Guilt by the conservative black economist Thomas Sowell. He recorded the book directly onto a Teac Cassette deck. During those first few years he worked an average of 100 hours per week, but at least he was with his wife and five kids as they grew up and took part in the business.

Some of his biggest coups over the years include getting the rights to record books by C.S. Lewis of Narnia fame, and the rights to record A Beautiful Mind and Catch Me If You Can – both of which had movie tie-ins which helped sales greatly. Then in 1995 he signed a digital distribution deal with Audible.com, which has produced millions in revenue since then.

What started with one book on tape has now mushroomed into a company that employs nearly 100 employees with thousands of recorded books in the form of CD's and MP3's you can download. They are now the first or second largest independently held audio book publisher in the world. Not bad for a "little home business"!

And by the way, they also rent their products to those who choose not to buy, adding further to their revenue stream. Craig fondly remembers those days at home:

"Those were great days and I will forever cherish the memories of working in the house and having the kids run from room to room interacting with our employees. I can recall my nephew Josh—when he was just 12—coming over and hanging out, challenging me to games of one-on-one basketball. Josh is now my key person and is very likely to become my successor. My son Alex, who is now 14, still begs to come into the office. So I think that because we ran the business out of the house for those several years, my family has become very attached and linked with the business. It's been wonderful." You can see Craig's web site at www.BlackstoneAudio.com

DVD & CD Duplication

Another friend of mine, Darryl Coulombe, who has done everything from cabinet making to selling flowers to being an EMT, fireman and dispatcher, now runs his own DVD and CD duplication business out of one small room in his home. What used to be a bedroom now looks something like a recording studio, with duplicating and recording equipment and monitors all over in every nook and cranny. He started his home business from scratch with one CD duplicator, and has gradually added more and more sophisticated editing and duplicating equipment so he can take care of a growing list of client. He transfers old recordings from records and cassettes to CD's, and also transfers old 8mm films and videocassettes to DVD's. Most of his clients come from the recommendations of other customers, so he does almost no advertising except for an ad in the Yellow Pages.

Here's what Darryl says about his home business: "I love the control working at home gives me. I enjoy the work, so it rarely feels like work. Some days the toughest decision I have to make is "do I answer the door in my slippers, or put on my shoes." Eat your heart out, corporate guys! You can check out Darryl's web site at www.creative-video-designs.com

Radio Spots and Promotional Audio

Curt Morse is an outstanding young man I have known since he was just a little guy. I once had him in a 5th grade Sunday School class, and was tempted to use weapons of mass destruction on him many times, as he crawled under tables and generally did his best to distract the rest of the class.

I'm really glad that I restrained myself, as that playful inquisitiveness in him turned out to be a great quality, and led him into a career as an MC and later a radio announcer. I'll let him tell the rest of the story on how his home business came about:

"Like many, I began working at home as a way to make extra income. I was working at a non-profit ministry in Colorado where the salaries were below average. I had a new family and a new mortgage and needed extra income to make ends meet.

I was an audio producer (focusing mainly on radio programs) and would receive various projects from time to time that would allow me to add to my income. In 1993 another non-profit group who asked me to help them with their own new radio program approached me. It was during this time that I first began working consistently at home (while also working at my full-time job aka – "my REAL job").

Later that year as things progressed and more projects came my way, it became apparent that I would need to choose between my full-time job and starting my own business. I chose the later in late 1994 and found working at home (in my basement) to be both satisfying and challenging.

It was satisfying because it was nice to be close to my family and to be available for them. With a wife and two young children (a 3 year old son and 1 year old daughter), I could see them all the time and choose my work hours when they were asleep. I am an early riser and many times I would get out of bed at 2:00am or 3:00am to begin work. Since I had a pretty short commute (just two flights of stairs downstairs – some times in my robe!), it was obviously convenient.

The challenging part for me was that I was learning how to run a business on the fly with little money in the bank. Many experts say that before you begin a business of your own, you should have 6-12 months salary in the bank (what planet is that person living on?) and to not expect a profit until after two years.

It is true that those first few years were pretty tough. In fact, I used to joke that I went from working at a non-profit company to running one! In spite of my shortcomings and with a lot of prayer and support from family, we survived. But I wanted to do more than just survive.

After a few years of working in my basement and adding some new clients to my new company, one of my clients offered to move me to Phoenix, Arizona to help him begin a new radio program. He really wanted me to come to work for him, but I told him that I was committed to growing my business and he agreed to hire me with that stipulation.

We began the moving process to Phoenix in 1996 and it turned out to be a great move. First, it gave me consistent monthly income (which I did not have before) and a chance to grow my business. I also became good friends with this client, and that friendship continues to this day.

On the negative side, I had to move my office outside of my home and pay rent (we moved from a good-sized home in Colorado to a two bedroom apartment in Phoenix).

That was tough for my wife and children and it also meant that I would not be able to see them as often since I was no longer working at home. My new project in Phoenix also turned out to take up quite a bit more time than what was estimated. I was working about 40 hours per week on this new project and another 50 hours per week with the rest of my business (I hadn't worked those kind of hours since I was in my early 20s). That meant that I saw even less of my family.

After about 17 months of working like this, I was able to build up enough clients to allow my wife and me to think about moving to the Pacific Northwest (which had been our goal for the last five years). We made the move to Bend, Oregon in 1998 and into a home with a large bonus room above my garage that would become my office.

So now I had come full circle with my business. I began my company in my home, moved it to an outside office and then back into my home again.

Since I have chosen to keep my business small with no employees (my company is Skynet Media Inc.), it is most convenient for me to work at home and adjust my hours to fit my schedule. I also hire "sub-contractors (writers, producers, editors, voice talent and others) to help me with projects. They appreciate the work and it keeps my overhead down. It is also rewarding to be able to work on the projects that I really want to work on and with clients I really want to work with. I feel blessed to be able to live where I want to live and work with the people that I want to work with."

Two Home Businesses in the Same Family - Bookkeeping & Underground Cameras

Another neighbor of mine who works at home is Laura Vaughn, who has a regular clientele who bring her their bookkeeping work. I see people drive into her driveway, take in a stack of papers, then some-time later drop back and pick up the finished product. She's an avid tennis player and enters tournaments all over the North West, so when she's not on the road backhanding little white balls around the court, she makes some extra income while letting her muscles rest between tourneys.

Her husband Dave is an expert in underground cameras, and does lots of work for municipal governments, peering underground with his special equipment to make sure water and sewer lines are behaving themselves. He operates his business out of his home too – but often he needs to travel to the city or county in question to train personnel in the use of his equipment. And since his work requires quite a bit of travel, Laura's home business keeps her active mind occupied while he's gone.

Web Template Designer

Andrea Thomson is a Canadian stay-at-home Mom who used to work for a large company in computer programming and design. Here is what she has to say about being able to work at home now:

"I feel very blessed to have the opportunity to work from home. No more commuting! No more child care costs! I can now set my hours around my family and their needs.

With three young children, ages 4, 7, and 11, it's key that my schedule fit around their busy school and after school schedules. I get up early most days - around 6:30am - so as to get a jumpstart on emails and some phone calls. It's amazing how much more you get done in a quiet house while everyone is sleeping. And, that first cup of coffee tastes better when you can sit and enjoy it rather than rushing to pack-up lunches and back-packs! Our youngest attends preschool every day for four hours and this is a huge helper in my schedule. It provides me with a solid block of time in which to attend to communication. After school time is devoted to normal family activities: sports, friends visiting, homework, prepping dinner. I can still keep a pulse on emails and phone calls if need be. After supper and the children's bedtime, I am regularly back to my desk to complete any work not finished during my fragmented day. On the odd occasion, work may demand that I pull an "all nighter". This is typically a late night - no later than 2:00am. Sure, it can hurt in the morning but nobody but the kids have to see my tired face and I'm not struggling in traffic to get to work.

Overall, it's a balancing act. It works for us and I have to say that anyone with a good sense of organization and the determination to make it work would enjoy the challenge and rewards of working from home."

You can see some of Andrea's templates available at http://www.goldenpinecone.com

Transcription

Another gal with a part-time home business to supplement the family income while raising 3 kids is Shirley Buckmaster. She and her husband Steve own Buckmaster Coffee Company, and Steve supplies his brand of coffee to many grocery stores in Oregon and Northern California. Shirley works about 3 mornings a week in her home office transcribing medical records for local doctors, which works out well between being a taxi Mom shuttling her kids to school, games, church and the like. Here's what she had to say about working at home:

"I decided to get involved with this field as I was home schooling my kids at the time and wanted to earn a little extra money to help pay the bills. I had no experience, other than I was a fast typist, but I learned on the job 12 years ago. I wouldn't necessarily recommend doing it that way. Even a basic medical terminology class would be most helpful, if not specific classes for medical transcribing.

Benefits include going to the fridge any time I want, taking a nap any time I want, sun tanning, et al. Seriously, freeing you up to be able to be involved with my kids or other activities is a huge blessing, as you don't have set hours as a contracted transcriptionist although I do have a 24 hour turn-around, so do have to have my tapes done by the next day. The pay is good, however, you are solely responsible for taxes and SS and there is no Worker's comp for injuries, which are downsides."

Selling on eBay

About umpteen zillion people work at home either part-time or full-time selling their wares on eBay. My brother Garland and his wife Roberta specialize in depression glass, and as they travel the country (they are retired) they stop at flea markets and antique shops and Goodwill and Salvation Army searching for items they can sell on eBay. Over the past 4 years or so they have sold over 4000 items, ranging from their specialty to baseball cards, comic books, tokens, and many other items greatly desired by collectors.

I could go on and on relating stories about folks like you and I who create their own home businesses. But you get the point. It can be done, and is being done by many, many people!

Chapter ③

How To Turn Your Knowledge & Skills Into a "1-Person-School" You Can Operate In Your Home, Then Grow It Into Something Much Larger!

It doesn't matter what your talents and skills are. Somewhere there is a hungry market for your skill. You just need to find that market and give them what they are looking for...your skill. Do you play guitar? There are about 19 zillion people in the world wishing they could "play like you." Do you play piano? Another gazillion folks are waiting for you to teach them what you know and can play. You can teach piano. I ought to know – I have operated a "one-man-music-school" in my home for many years, and taught many others to do the same.

But what if you play the sax or flute or trumpet or drums or are a singer? What if you do none of the above, but know how to balance a checkbook, or know how to create beautiful scrapbooks, or have skills in cartooning or needlepoint or camera repair or... It doesn't matter...millions of people want to learn what you know!

Maybe there won't be tons of people in your hometown who want to learn what you know, or do what you do, but get out into the mail order market and you'll discover more than you ever thought. Get out into the internet, and there's virtually no limit – people who want to learn what you know are coming online faster than you could possibly imagine –knowledge-hungry people from all over the world...China, India, Peru, France, Canada....on and on. It's absolutely astounding –

something like 100,000 people per day get online for the first time –
and many of them are looking for what you have to offer!

But don't start with the internet. Instead, start with your own "Your-
Name Local School" where you create your own instructional material to teach a few students. Then later add your own "Your-Name
Mail Order School" Use your newly created instructional material to
teach "long distance" to a vast student body. When that's going, then
add "Your-Name World-Wide-Web School"

"Duane, That would be great, but how do I get started?" I'm glad
you asked, because you came to the right place to find out how.

I've done all 3 – starting with teaching just one student, I now have
taught hundreds of thousands of people all over the world. And starting with one little 8-page manual on the subject of reading music, I
now have well over 500 instructional DVD's, CD's, books, cassettes,
charts, and videos – all designed to help people play the piano better
and understand music better.

I started out as a "One-man music school"; later added a "One
man music mail order school"; and then about 8 years ago added
a "One-man world-wide-web music school". (You can go see it right
now if you want to at www.playpiano.com)

For years I taught students in person, in my "One-Man-Music-
School", and made an excellent living doing it. Then I discovered a
way to "multiply myself" so I could teach many people at the same
time instead of just one. Some people call it "mail order", but I just
called it great! By printing my lessons & recording them on cassette
tape or video, then later on CD's and DVD's, I could not only reach
a lot more people, but I could teach anywhere – and I do. Farmers
in Montana, Doctors in Florida, CPA's in Washington, Barbers in
Texas, Housewives in Kentucky – you name it. Instead of having 100

students, you can have thousands! I presently have over 80,000 people who subscribe to my newsletter, and I have a young friend named Jermaine in the same business who has 4 times that many! And another great and talented friend named Dave in my own home town that is cleaning my clock when it comes to marketing savy and technical facility. Am I worried? Not in the least. The demand for instruction is growing at a geometrical rate, so there is plenty of room for all of us. Not only that, we can co-operate together and work out affiliate relationships that benefit us all.

Turn Your Teaching Into Many Products

You too can turn your personal teaching into books, charts, games, cassettes, videos, DVD's, CD's, software and more. You can market them through mail order catalogs, classified ads, free write-ups, direct mail, and a wide variety of other outlets. Space doesn't permit to cover all the details of selling by mail order and direct mail, but many fine books are available on the subject at your local library, and a few days spend immersing yourself in them will get you up and running sooner than you may think. It's not near as hard as you might think – I've been doing it for almost 30 years now, and have sold hundreds of thousands of music and piano courses. There's no reason at all why you can't do it too!

Your Own Web Site

Your own web site is the next logical step once you have your mail order business going, and underwear is the preferred clothing, except of course when you take your orders to the Post Office and your checks to the bank. If you do it right – and I'll show you how to do that – your business can literally EXPLODE, since millions of people will be seeing your web site. It used to be difficult to get a web site up and running, but no more. I'll tell you about several programs you can use to create a beautiful site quickly and inexpensively.

Once you have your teaching business in place, and have created some lessons of your own on video or books or charts or DVD's or CD's and have learned to market them by mail order, it is time to explode your teaching business even more by creating your own web site and making your teaching available to people all over the world! You can even teach online if you want – I don't choose to do that, but a friend of mine does, and it works well for him. And now we have computer discs and CD's and DVD's and interactive media of various sorts – all of which can contain your music ideas and lessons – and who knows what will develop in the next few years. The person who starts now and begins to get into this media – the super information highway – will have a giant head start on others.

How Much Can You Earn?

So how much money can you earn in your home business teaching what you know? The key word in that title is "earn". You and I both know that money doesn't grow on guitars or computers. We have to earn it before we get to keep it, home business or not. But given that, here are some estimates based on my own experience and others in the teaching business field that I know or know about. This applies not just to teaching music, but to teaching anything. I just use music as an example since that's the field with which I am most familiar.

It depends on what part of the country you live in, and whether or not you live in the city or in the country, as rates are dramatically different from place to place. But as an average a beginning music teacher could expect to earn about $25. per lesson, and if you teach half-hour lessons, that is $50. per hour. Experienced teachers can and do often earn twice that – $50. per lesson – $100. per hour. And a few top teachers earn a great deal more than that, as you might suppose. Let me give you a scenario that might spark an idea in your mind: Instead of charging by the lesson, charge by the month. That way you stabilize your income by eliminating cancellations and make up lessons. For example, back in the 70's I charged by the month, and students would come for an hour lesson instead of a half-hour lesson, which greatly appealed to parents. I broke the hour up into 3 segments: the student would spend 20 minutes with me, 20 minutes watching a film strip about music theory, and 20 minutes with one of my older students working on what I had assigned them. They loved it, and it worked out well for everyone – the student, the parents, and me. That way I had 3 students onboard each hour, rotating between the 3 "stations" mentioned above, so I was taking in 3 times the income a normal teacher would take in during the same time period! Of course I paid my "assistant teachers" (older students) something, plus I had to buy the film strips and projector to get going, but once in motion, it was an excellent home business income for a minimum of time spent teaching music. I carried about 100 students during those years, but only taught between the hours of 3PM to 8PM 5 days a week – that's just 25 hours per week – but made a full time income from it, plus had my days free to develop the second part of my teaching endeavors – the mail order division, which in time far eclipsed the private teaching element.

So if YOU set up the same program as I had back in the 70's, instead of charging $35. per month, you could easily charge 3 times that – after all, this is the 21st century – not 1974 – and you may have noticed that things cost just a bit more now! (I bought a brand new Toyota Corolla back then for $1995.! Think what they cost now, then extrapolate that to your teaching income.... So let's say that you charge $100. per month and you have 3 students per hour (like I did), and teach from 3 to 8 PM five days a week (like I did). That's 25 teaching hours times 3 students = 75 students times $100. per student = $7500. per month, which figures out to be about $75. per hour. Better than a part-time job at Burger Bash, I would say. And you still have all morning and the early part of the afternoon to build other parts of your business.

Well, you get the idea. Now take inventory of your skills and what you love to do most, then get started. An exciting life awaits!

Chapter 4

How to Work At Home Even If You Don't Have a Product or Service of Your Own.

Did you know that many people all over the world work at home, yet don't even have their own product or service? Because of the growth of the internet, an entire community of people have been formed called "affiliate marketers". Affiliate marketing is a commision-based business opportunity. You advertise and promote products, and receive commissions.

When I first heard about affiliate marketing, my reaction was "What else is new? People have been acting as dealers and distributors for companies for hundreds of years. What makes affilate marketing so special?" Way back in the 70's I had "dealers" who advertised my music courses in various ways – ads, classified ads, mailings, etc – and we "drop-shipped" for them. When they got an order from their advertising efforts, they would send us a shipping label with the customer's name on it along with a check for 50% of the price of the course they sold. We would then package the course, slap on the shipping label, and drop the course in the mail. The customer figured it came from the person who sold it. Very neat system, and it's still done today by some firms.

Affiliate marketing is like that, except instead of selling the product, you simply "point" prospects at the web site of the company you represent, and they take it from there.

They do all the:

- *Selling*
- *Collecting payment*
- *Shipping the product*
- *Customer support*

Which means that you have:

- *No inventory*
- *No investment in products*
- *No selling*
- *No shipping*
- *No customer support*

Sounds like a deal to me.

So if you, as the affiliate, don't have to do any selling, stocking products, shipping to the customer, or answering their questions about the product, what in the heck DO you do? Sounds like the world's cushiest job to me.

Well, it is in many ways. But that means that you have to be really good at the few things you DO have to do, which include:

Getting traffic to your site (or the site you represent as an affiliate).

You do this basically three ways:

1) *Search engine optimization*
2) *Publicity via article writing and press releases*
3) *Pay per click campaigns.*

Pre-selling that traffic in a way that makes them want to "click-through" to your merchant. You do this by writing helpful articles about the products you represent, and/or using audio and video on your site to tell about your products.

Capturing the name and e-mail address of those folks who come to your site. You do this by using either a "squeeze page" or a pop-up or an opt-in box on your site.

Following them up with interesting and enticing e-mails that make them want to come back to your site or the site of the merchant you represent. You can do this by subscribing to an auto-responder service and then sending out a series of helpful e-mails on a sequential basis – daily, weekly, or whatever. An alternate to this is using RSS, all of which will be explained later in this book.

It is a unique field because of the incredible power of the internet to reach people from every walk of life all over the world.

Just like other commission-based businesses, you have to get your message in front of potential clients. Instead of advertising in the newspaper or on television, or calling clients on the telephone, the affiliate marketer primarily builds a business online, and places an inordinate emphasis on the search engine results and placement, either through advertising or other means.

This type of business has unique benefits. There is no customer support. You should begin with very small capital investments in order to learn the business without financial risk. You have no physical inventory. You will have access to ads provided by merchants. It takes time to learn the skills, but the industry is so new that the only way to learn it is on the Internet.

If you begin small, practice, and learn from your mistakes, you can become very profitable. Commission Junction, one of the largest affiliate networks which will be discussed in this guidebook, has extra awards for those affiliates who earn more than $10,000 a month. You can earn much more or a whole lot less than that – like nothing at all –it depends on you. The tools are in place, but you have to make it happen. The opportunity is available today, and it is growing leaps and bounds. Some affiliates earn extra spending money while holding down another job. Some stay-at-home Moms supplement their family income through affiliate marketing. And then there are "super affiliates" such as James Martell and Rosalind Gardiner who make more per month than most people make all year. Rosalind wrote a book about her affiliate experiences titled "The Super-Affiliate Handbook". Her book is described this way:

"It tells the amazing true story of how one woman who was an air traffic controller for many years, with no previous business experience, earns $435,000+ per year selling other people's stuff online! In her down-to-earth, sincere and often humorous style, Rosalind Gardner guides you through the entire process of building an affiliate marketing business on the 'Net. In 236 pages, and more than 68,000 words, you'll learn how to pick the best programs, negotiate a commission raise and save time, money and effort on everything from affiliate software to web hosting."

Here is how she describes the experience: "For 20 years before starting my Internet business, I worked for the government, as an air traffic controller. I knew I wasn't going to make it to retirement in that occupation. The crazy shifts were making me sick, so I had to do something to secure my future so that I could quit before the job killed me. Fortunately, right around the time I fell ill, I got connected to the 'Net. I'm no genius, but it didn't take long before I saw the potential for a fun and lucrative home-based business using the 'Net. I was right.

Two years after I started to 'play' with web sites, I quit my job as an air traffic controller. When I quit my day job in 2000, my sites were raking in $30,000 to 50,000 US dollars **EACH** and **EVERY** month. In 2002, I earned a whopping $436,797 affiliating with Internet merchants and selling their products. In 2003 and 2004, I earned much more than that!" You can check out one of her sites at www.superaffiliatehandbook.com

James Martell, still another super-affiliate and author of "Affiliate Marketers Handbook" is a modest guy and doesn't broadcast his earnings, but I happen to know that he earns double or triple what an average doctor earns – somewhere in the neighborhood of six figures per month, which is a pretty nice neighborhood. Of course, he has been at it for several years now, and owns about 100 affiliate sites on subjects ranging from babies to baseball. You can read all about his success in the affiliate marketing field at www.affiliate-marketers-guide.com

So while there is absolutely no guarantee, it obviously can be done. Here is just a tiny sampling of the **BIG** brand-name companies that use affiliate programs to promote their products online:

- American Express
- Discover
- Hickory Farms
- Cingular
- Dell
- Gap
- Overstock
- Amazon
- Old Navy
- E-Toys
- Eddie Bauer
- Coldwater Creek
- Delta
- EBay
- Wal Mart
- Musician's Friend
- Barnes & Nobel
- Weight Watchers

...and on and on – thousands of merchants waiting anxiously for people to represent them.

Entire networks like Commission Junction, Linkshare and BeFree have been built solely to administer online merchants' affiliate programs. Basically, any company trying to do business on the web WITHOUT an affiliate program nowadays, is dead in the water.

Affiliate Networks to Join

For companies to manage an in-house affiliate program, it can an expensive, logistical nightmare. Some companies create and manage their own affiliate programs, but the largest, most lucrative programs are outsourced to "affiliate networks" such as the ones listed below. When you are starting out as an affiliate network member ("publisher"), these programs are the most important ones to join.

Essential Affiliate Networks

ClickBank "http://clickbank.com" has over 100,000 affiliates that exclusively marketing digital products and ClickBank itself. ClickBank's categories for its products as of this writing are include B2B, Computing, Entertainment, Fitness, Money, Society, and many more.

Commission Junction "http://www.cj.com" is the leading affiliate network on the planet, and today includes some of the products that were developed by BeFree before that affiliate network was purchased by ValueClick. The company provides a suite of tools to help publishers measure return on investment and to manage their marketing efforts. Some well-known CJ affiliates are NextTag®, Ebates®, UPromise®, and Lycos® They also host an annual seminar for affiliate marketers in their home town, Santa Barbara, California. If you ever have a chance to go, be sure to take it in, as you will learn a lot as well as make contacts with companies you might what to represent as an affiliate.

LinkShare "http://www.linkshare.com" was the pioneer and is the other leading affiliate program, with over 10 million partnerships. Some of its advertisers include Wal-mart, American Express, Hotwire, and others.

Selecting Programs

The first and most important criteria for selecting a merchant to represent is to ask yourself "What excites me? What would I love to own myself? What product could I enthusiastically recommend to others?" All other criteria pale in comparison, because if you don't love the subject, you're not going to promote or write about it with the fire it takes to pre-sell a product or service.

Having said that, explore the listings of companies with which you can partner, looking especially for the following characteristics to help you sign up to be a partner:

- *Programs with the highest "Earnings Per Click" (EPC)*
- *Programs with the highest payout per sale*
- *Programs with the highest payouts throughout the network ("Network Earnings")*
- *Programs with the highest all-time payouts*
- *Products about which you are particularly knowledgeable or interested*
- *New programs (which will have less competition)*

Not all affiliate networks will necessarily provide the same information. When they do, they may use their own terminology which you will need to learn by studying the help files. You would learn in Commission Junction's help files that EPC is actually earnings per one-hundred clicks. Over at ClickBank, you would find that the term for this is "Gravity." Become acquainted with the help files.

The best way to start is to get your feet wet with with one or two programs. Sign up as an affiliate member and take a look the materials available to you for marketing their site. Signing up to be an affiliate of a particular company is known as joining or applying to a "Program"; in other words, your application could be rejected due to innapropriate content. If you are accepted, you will receive HTML code that you can paste into your Web pages. You may also receive an ongoing merchandising information.

Many Partners, One Check

Visit the affiliate networks listed above, and sign up as an affiliate member with the top three. Later you may want to join the remaining networks depending on your interests or if a particular company is available through one of the other sites. You may receive commissions from Dell® computer, Overstock.com®, the New York Times® Discover Card®, and dozens of other companies and only join the three leading programs. Best of all, those checks will not come directly from the various partner sites, but from the affiliate network sites.

Chapter 5

Tell The World About Your Product By Writing Articles for the Web!

Writing and submitting articles is one the fastest ways to bring people to your website. You can get lots of targeted visitors to your site without spending a penny on advertising. Thanks to new distribution channels, you can get visitors to your site within just a few days – weeks at the most.

For example, if you had a web site on fishing, you could write short articles about various aspects of fishing and submit. Here is an example of one person who publicizes his fishing site by writing articles about his adventures in fishing: http://ezinearticles.com/?expert=A.J._Klott

And another by a person (me) who publicizes his piano courses by writing articles about piano playing: http://ezinearticles.com/?expert=Duane_Shinn

Here are just a few of the benefits:

1) *It costs nothing. You can write and submit short articles of from 300 to 500 words -- one typed page -- to all of the following article directories at no cost:*

http://www.goarticles.com
http://www.ezinearticles.com
http://www.ideamarketers.com
http://www.ideamarketers.com

http://biz-whiz.com

http://www.articlecity.com

http://www.thewhir.com/find/articlecentral

http://www.contentdesk.com

http://www.freetraffictip.com/members

http://www.marketing-seek.com

http://www.family-content.com

http://www.addme.com/nlsubmit.htm

http://www.netterweb.com/artcls

http://www.isnare.com/login.php

http://www.valuablecontent.com

http://www.internetbasedmoms.com

http://www.powerhomebiz.com/termsofuse

http://www.sbinformation.about.com

http://www.workoninternet.com/Submit_Article.html

http://www.constant-content.com/presignup/1

http://www.allfreelancework.com/submitarticles.php

http://www.article-emporium.com

http://www.businessknowhow.com/newsletter

http://www.buzzle.com

http://www.impactarticles.com

http://www.certificate.net/wwio/ideas.shtml

http://www.webpronews.com/submit.html

http://www.web-source.net/syndicator_submit.htm

http://articles.simplysearch4it.com/articlesub.php

http://www.storebuilder.co.uk/submitcontent.html

http://www.articlesfactory.com

http://searchwarp.com

http://www.ezau.com/latest/articles/0127.shtml

http://www.allthewebsites.org/articles

http://www.advertisingknowhow.com

2) *Articles which are helpful, funny, or just interesting are much more powerful than ads. Using the article submission technique you can sometimes get your web site listed on dozens or even hundreds of web sites within a very short time. You don't have to pay to put your article on these sites or even provide a reciprocal link -- the site owners add your article to their site because it contains content of interest to their readers.*

3) *A link to your site will always appear in the resource box at the end of the article. This will give you a one-way incoming link. The higher the page rank of the site featuring your article, the better. Some news sites carry a PR of 7, 8, or even 9. Landing an article on one of these sites is priceless -- free advertising at it's very best.*

4) *The search engines such as MSN, Yahoo, & Google spider your articles, so make sure they contain the keywords important to your site. A keyword rich article has a very good chance of getting ranked in the search engines thereby exposing your web site link to searchers, as well as article readers.*

For more continuing information on writing articles for internet distribution, sign up for Chris Knight's blog on the subject. He is the owner of EzineArticles.com, and extremely knowledgeable on the subject. Go to http://ezinearticles.com/blog/ to sign up for his free blog.

Here's one article I wrote and distributed across the web:

Killer Piano Playing Secrets of a Chord Addict! - By Duane Shinn

I wish you could have seen me play the piano when I was just learning. I was the nearest thing to "hopeless" that you could imagine. I was into baseball, not music – and my heroes were Joe DiMaggio, Mickey Mantle, and Ted Williams. (And by the way, I still have a picture of those 3 guys on my wall.) My dream was to hit baseballs like them, not to play the piano.

But an opportunity to play with a combo presented itself to me when I was a freshman in high school. Seems the piano player of the group had graduated the previous year, and nobody else played piano well enough to play in the school jazz combo. I didn't know zilch about playing in a group, and I didn't know chords. But I was excited to have the opportunity to play with older guys, and so I took the job.

The lead sax player told me I really should know chords in order to play in the group, so I searched through a music magazine until I found an ad for a chord chart. It cost two bucks, as I recall, so I sent off for it. When I received it in the mail I slipped it behind the keys on my parents old upright piano, and promptly learned to play my first chord – Dm7. I LOVED the sound of it, and was hooked for life on chords. The 2nd chord I learned was Cmaj7, then Em7, then Ebm7 – and before that first night was over I had learned to play "Frankie & Johnnie" – the tune in my right hand, and those fabulous 7th chords in my left hand!

I loved it – LOVED IT – LOVED IT! And it even sounded good enough to impress some of my friends the next day. I suppose that simple chord chart that cost me two bucks has been worth several million over the course of my lifetime. And much more than that, has been worth quadrillions in pleasure and satisfaction and relaxation and...Even though I came in the back door as far as piano playing was concerned, I learned fast because of what I knew about chords, so college was a snap, and so was my post-graduate Masters Degree at Southern Oregon University. After high school I studied with several of the finest private teachers on the West Coast, including a year with THE finest teacher – his name was Dave – and his studio was on Cauhenga Blvd. in Hollywood. As I would come for my piano lesson, I would often pass a big name recording artist coming to their lesson – and anyone who was anyone in Hollywood in those days took lessons from Dave.

Dave taught me 2 fundamental principles about piano playing:
1) *The piano is NOT played with the hands – it is played with the brain. The hands are just tools.*
2) *If you master chord relationships, you can master music.*

I've got little fat hands with short fingers. Hardly the ideal hands for piano playing. I've also got a lousy sense of rhythm. But you know what? Because of those two principles Dave taught me, I can play "above" my fat hands and my weak rhythm.
Above?
Yes.
Above.
Once a person "gets into the flow" of understanding chord relationships and then letting the brain knowledge flow into the hands, that person plays "above" his ability.

And the great thing about it is this: It's not some secret formula hidden in the archives of some dusty music conservatory in Prague. Instead it's an open book – there are courses galore on the internet you can take for peanuts compared to a traditional music conservatory. The internet age has provided a way for the average person to become an above-average musician!

Duane Shinn is the author of over 500 music and piano books and products such as DVD's, CD's, musical games for kids, chord charts, musical software, and piano lesson instructional courses for

43

adults. He holds advanced degrees from Southern Oregon University and was the founder of Piano University in Southern Oregon. He can be reached at http://www.pianolessonsbyvideo.com. He is the author of the popular free 101-week e-mail newsletter titled "Amazing Secrets Of Piano Chords & Sizzling Chord Progressions" with over 55,000 current subscribers. The article can be found at http://ezinearticles.com/?What-In-The-World-Would-We-Do-Without-Music?&id=73069

Then after you get the hang of it, go thou and do likewise. A world of free publicity is just waiting for you to claim it!

Chapter 6

How To Get An Avalanche Of Free Publicity For Your Home Business!

A press release –sometimes also known as a news release - is an easy and low-cost method of getting word about your product or service out to the public. With the advent of the internet, it is easier than ever to write and distribute press releases all over the world for next to nothing – sometimes literally nothing, and other times for just a minimum fee.

Back in the early days of our home business we used press releases to get free write-ups in magazines and newspapers all over the country, from Popular Mechanics to House Beautiful to Sheet Music Magazine to the Portland Oregonian and hundreds of others. We even got a news release on the front page of the Wall Street Journal along side a picture of Robert Redford. My friends in Medford even started me calling me "Robert Redford" as a friendly joke for the next year or two.

There are many ways you can get tons of free publicity in the form of write-ups in magazines, newspapers, and even radio and TV. And sometimes you can turn family events into human-interest stories that editors like and will publish in their magazine and newspapers.

One way is to compose a printed news release on your product or service, but include a story involving your family into the release. Write the release like a news article in a newspaper. Tell who, what, when, why, and how interested people can benefit from your product. Avoid hard selling copy — just give the facts, and if you can weave in an interesting story in the process, all the better.

Human Interest News Stories Make Great Press Releases

For example, I am a musician with a line of products in the music educational field. Years ago I created a giant musical staff out of plastic and turned it into a game that kids could play on the floor. In the news release about it, I told how my own kids used it, and included some dialog between them:

"That's a whole note!" exclaimed my daughter Kendra.

"Is not! It's got a stem, and whole notes don't have stems" my son Kurt corrected her.

"Is too!"

"Is not!"

"Is too!"

"Is not!"

"Oh...what's a stem, Kurt?"

"It's the line coming down from the note head, stupid."

"I am not stupid!"

"Are too!"

"Am not!"

Finally Mom intervened before an all-out war broke out.

But henceforth and evermore both of my kids knew the difference between a whole note and a half note.

For some reason, editors found that little story amusing, and wrote up the story pretty much as I sent it in. They also included information on how interested parents could get a "Giant Staff Game" for their own kids, and as a result we got orders from all over the states and some foreign countries from both parents and schools. It was written up in House Beautiful, Better Homes & Gardens, plus many music magazines and teachers' journals.

This was not just a one-time fluke, either – over the years we received news write-ups galore in everything from the Wall Street Journal to Popular Mechanics – all related to our product, but written in a way to make editors smile and then decide to publish the release in their publications.

Can you do the same? Think about the funny little incidents in your family life, and then think of ways you can work that into a news release about your product or service.

Ad agencies would like you to believe that mere mortals like you and I have no business in the publicity field – it should be left to professionals like them, at horrendous fees. If you're Ford or Coke or Nike, great. But if you're an individual working out of your home trying to promote a product on your own, you have no choice but to do it yourself.

My mentor, Joe Cossman, author of "How I Made a Million Dollars In Mail Order", used to tell a story about an ad agency that quoted him a price of $50,000. to achieve certain publicity goals that he had in mind. He then told the agency that he had already achieved those goals himself at a cost of less than $500.

If I walked into an agency today and asked them how much it would cost for them to get me a write-up in the following publications and web sites, how much do you think it would cost?

- Yahoo news
- The Portland Oregonian
- Mississippi Educational Advance
- Cappers Weekly
- Parade

- Wall St Journal (front page)
- The Medford Mail Tribune
- Farm Journal
- Grit
- Popular Mechanics

- Opportunity Magazine
- Sheet Music Magazine
- Music Educators Journal
- Harmonizer

- Entrepreneur
- Clavier
- Sing Out

...And over 500 other magazines, newspapers, newsletters, ezines and web sites.

The answer is – they would laugh me right out of the agency, because they couldn't begin to guarantee such coverage in the first place, and if they could, it would cost a medium-size fortune. And yet I have gotten all those write-ups (plus radio interviews and a couple TV interviews) by myself – no advertising agency involved, just by sending out news releases.

And it used to be much harder and more time consuming and expensive than it is today, since it involved printing the release, inserting it in an envelope, paying the postage, and so on. Today it's a snap: It can all be done at your computer by using the internet services listed at the end of this chapter.

The advantages of press releases are obvious:
1) You get to write the release yourself, so you can say whatever you want to say about your product or service.
2) They are quick. It's not unusual to send out a press release and have it picked up the same day by a wire service or internet news feed.
3) You can get worldwide exposure for pennies.

With the development of the world-wide web, even home businesses now have a convenient way to submit their press releases to thousands of magazines and web sites and writers and news papers with the click of a mouse. Press release distribution services are becoming increasingly popular for both web-based and real-world based businesses.

How to Write a Press Release

If you were a newspaper reporter, you would be trained to ask the "5 W's": Who, what, where, when & why. Writing a good news release is no different – you need to answer all those questions in the body of your release. If you don't answer those 5 questions, your release will be incomplete and probably will be ignored by editors who receive many such releases every day. The easier you make it for the editor, the easier it becomes for your news release to be published.

Here's a news release I wrote in about an hour and sent out via a service called PRWeb. Notice the headline sums up the story in a concise fashion, while the body copy fleshes out the summary in terms of the 5 W's:

Headline:

New E-book Published on 'Secrets of Exciting Chords & Chord Progressions'

Summary:

PlayPiano.com today announced the publication of a new e-book titled "Secrets of Exciting Chords & Chord Progressions" with links to 40 web pages which demonstrate each chord & progression in full-color photos and narrated sound. The book covers all major, minor, diminished and augmented chords, plus many extensions such as 7ths and 9ths, plus chord progressions and how they work.

Body copy:

(PRWEB) January 4, 2006 – Despite the popularity of music in general and piano playing in particular, most adults who took piano lessons when they were kids did not continue with their playing and as a result play either very little or not at all.

The reasons for this are usually expressed as "I hated to practice", or "my piano teacher was so strict", or "I had to play all those scales and never got to learn the songs I really wanted to play." The bottom line, though, was simply that the student for one reason or another never learned the structure of music – chords and chord progressions – and so never really understood the music they were trying to read.

Duane Shinn, the author of the new e-book, experienced the same thing until he discovered chords when he was 14. He had taken piano lessons as a child, but didn't really find music exciting until he had a chance to play with the high school dance band. To join the band, he had to learn chords – and learn them in a hurry. He sent off for a $2. chord chart that he saw advertised in Popular Mechanics, and from that little chart he learned the three most important chords in any key, in any song.

That little $2 chord chart led to a long career in music, a degree from Southern Oregon University, a teaching studio named Piano University and eventually the founding of http://www.PlayPiano.com – a web site dedicated to teaching adults how to understand and play music using chords and chord progressions.

Duane says about this new e-book, "Everyone knows about the "front door" to piano playing – learning to read music and practice scales and so on, but there really is a "backdoor" to piano playing, too. It's not necessarily better than the front door, but for adults who want to start playing the songs they love, it's much faster and more fun, since you understand what you are doing right from square one."

Complete information about "Secrets of Exciting Chords & Chord Progressions" can be found at http://www.piano-music-lessons.com.

This simple news release was read 23,226 times, picked up by 530 news sources, and downloaded 47 times as a PDF. Not bad for a home-made press release! Go thou and do likewise.

Here's a list of some of the places online where you can distribute your press release:

- Express-press-release.com
- I-Newswire.com
- OpenPR.com
- Press411.com
- Pressbox.co.uk
- PR9.net
- PRWeb.com

- Free-press-release.com
- OnlinePressReleases.com
- Press-world.com
- PressReleaseSpider.com
- ClickPress.com
- PRLeap.com
- PRfree.com

There are others, but if you put these into action I think you'll be pleasantly surprised at the results!

Chapter ⑦

How To Get Your Own Powerful Web Site Up and Running Quickly

Launching a Web site is much easier today than in the past. It's easier because there are powerful tools available that replaces much of the coding with a visual interface. Here is a quick overview of options for creating your pages.

Hire a Designer

If you hire a professional designer to create a site, you can expect to pay at minimum $200. and possibly into the thousands. That's not necessarily bad–the professional is able to get results.

Here is a quick introduction to the ins and outs of hiring a Web designer. The ideal situation is to work with someone who has done exactly what you are trying to accomplish. If you see a site that is similar to what you are trying to accomplish, try to find a design credit and contact the designer. Ask people at your company who they have worked with.

Some designers want to have total management of the site for a fee. You will want to revise your site, adding content and ads, on an ongoing basis. Therefore, creating an editable site, or simply providing templates that you can fill in, is often the best approach.

When you are trying to save money, you are likely to try to cut corners by hiring students, new designers, teenagers, or your son or daughter who has some ability to do such things. Be aware that the result is likely to be sporadic. If you are willing to let the person learn while they design, this may be acceptable.

When talking to a designer, ask:

- *Have they created web sites before?*
- *How will you edit the site once it is created?*
- *What is included in the design.*
- *Other questions. Designers have knowledge about Web hosting, Web domains, and so on. If you are confused about these topics, this can be a great learning opportunity.*

Hiring a Designer Online

Some resources available to help you with design work are Elance.com "www.elance.com" and LogoWorks "www.logoworks.com". Elance is an online marketplace (owned by eBay) where designers will bid on your project. LogoWorks is a company that will assign a team of designers to your logo design for a few hundred dollars.

Purchase a Web Template

Rather than hiring a designer, you can also purchase a design into which you then type articles, insert ads, and so on. Many companies sell templates. The best I have found is Golden Pine Cone. Check out their site at www.goldenpinecone.com

Use Page Creation Software

With Web page creation software, you will edit your site on your local computer. Presumably, you will then upload your site pages to a server at a hosting company. This means that you have two copies of your site. Some of the leading applications are listed below. In each case, expect to invest some study time of packages and options to select the best match of features to your needs. For tutorials of each of the products, just visit the sites below.

XSitePRO

XSitePro is a site creation tool promoted as the ultimate tool for web site design. The approach is to allow you to create sites as quickly as possible that look professional and are optimized for search engines. To that end, wizards, forms, and templates guide the user through design, keywords, and the insertion of Google Adsense and affiliate ads. An easy way to learn about the program is to view screenshots and introductory video on the site www.xsitepro.com/pr-resources.html

Dreamweaver®

Macromedia® (now an Adobe® company) released Dreamweaver in the 1990s. Since then, it has continued to be one of the visual design tools of choice. It is notable for "round-trip-trip HTML," which eliminates much redundant code during design, great template functions, a convenient site manager, and good compatibility across browsers. Like all the other visual applications, this one produces some bloated code. As of this writing, Dreamweaver 8 is the current version, and is available for a $199 upgrade and $399 new purchase. Once a template is edited, any changes to the template affects all pages which are based on it. A library of items can be populated with custom code snippets that automatically change within the site pages whenever the master library item is changed. Windows® and Macintosh® versions available. See the Macromedia site at www.macromedia.com

HomeSite®

A long-term favorite among code-oriented Web professionals, Home-Site presents all the code in a convenient tabbed interface. As of this writing, a free download is available from the Macromedia® website, but no price is listed (the previous price was $99). A light-weight version of HomeSite is built into Dreamweaver for directly editing the code. See the Macromedia site. http://www.macromedia.com

Microsoft® Frontpage®

For many users of Microsoft® Office®, this product will already reside on their hard drive. If you like the way Microsoft applications work, this may be a good fit for you. The application provides good visual design tools, good templating which happens to be compatible with Dreamweaver templates, and good site management. As of this writing, Frontpage 2003 has a retail price of $200 and an upgrade price of $70. See the Microsoft site at www.microsoft.com

RapidWeaver

A new Macintosh-only Web creation application that is intended to allow anyone to create professional-looking websites in minutes. There is no code-level editing with RapidWeaver, that is performed for you by the program. The application is versatile enough to allow development of business sites, blogs, photo galleries, podcasting, and more. Without bothering with coding, you can have code-compliant sites that include XHTML and CSS. The application comes with over 20 themes but allows mixing and matching of themes for hundreds of combinations. The Smart Publishing feature (common to other tools as well) detects which files have changed and only uploads those. Files that include PHP scripting are rendered live on your desktop, without the need to install a separate Web server and PHP package on your local machine. The Podcasting feature allows drag-and-drop placement of an audio file, and RapidWeaver will automatically update the site's RSS feed for the new file. Macintosh® only. Retails for less than $50. Visit the site for more information www.realmacsoftware.com/rapidweaver

Site Build-It

Site Build-It is an all-in-one solution that guarantees you traffic to your site. If the typical hosting company provides the equivalent of a blank slate, the SBI solution is more like a pre-printed form that you get to fill in. The SBI philosophy of making money online is "CTPM"–Content - Traffic - PreSell - Monetize. This leaves little room for the drudgery of coding sites. THerefore, wizards guide you through the process of inputting your information into the system, selecting the design, entering the keywords, adding affiliate links, and adding copy. Web-based services are at the ready, including newsletter registration and sending, "auto-responder" services (see chapter 5), site navigation, reciprocal link exchange tool (see chapter 4), search engine submissions, and more. Compared to typical blank-slate hosting, SBI hosting is expensive. However, they elminate all need to be a Web desiger, graphic artist, or Web coder. They also have impressive results, with a random survey of 1000 SBI sites ranking in the top 3% of all sites online, according to Alexa traffic ranking. SBI also offers a lucrative affiliate program and a pre-set site that you can link to. The advantages of the service are independently verified results, a coherent integrated system that is easily understood, and a system that works for anyone who can write content, rather than code sites. On the downside is a certain amount of hype on the site, and a high price in comparison to standard hosting. www.sitesell.com

Squarespace

This general-purpose Web-based site tool is perfect for anyone who wants an attractive, compliant site without focusing on technical knowledge. The site offers multiple ways to edit, automatic site structuring, dynamic layout, and powerful blogging options along with strong anti-spam features, which are as important in commentable site areas as it is for your e-mail. You can have secure member areas, and members can subscribe for updates whenever a page changes. Traffic analysis is included in the service, integrated support, and various publishing options such as printable articles, e-mail article links, XML syndication, and podcasting. All content can be spell checked online. As of this writing, Squarespace subscriptions range from $7 to $17 per month, depending on your needs. Visit Squarespace for more information - www.squarespace.com

Hosting and Domain Names

Even if you have your pages, you need to host your pages and assign a domain name. If you'll go to www.GoDaddy.com you can see if a domain name that you might like is available. A detailed treatment of those topics is beyond the scope of this book, but if will type in "web hosting" into a Google or Yahoo search box, you will find many companies that are anxious to host your web site. My sites are hosted by a local company called Ccountry, which makes it convenient when I need help. If you are new to the internet, it probably would be a good idea to find someone locally that can help you set up your site as well as host it for you.

Chapter 8

How To Use The Power Of Google, Yahoo & MSN To Let People Know About You & Your Product or Service

As you are well aware, change is happening in our society at break-neck speed. We are in a parabolic upswing of technology develop-ment never before experienced in the entire history of the world. Moore's Law, formulated by Gordon Moore of Intel and thought to be an exaggeration back in the 1970's, is now an understatement of change which applies not only to how much data can be stored in a computer chip, but in virtually every area of technology. It is reliably estimated that over 90% of the scientists who have ever lived are alive right now! How can this be?

Today thousands of brilliant scientists are graduating from colleges and universities all over the world – China, India, Japan, Korea, etc. – and they all have computers and they all share knowledge with other scientists all over the world at the speed of light. So they are not only standing on the shoulders of scientists gone before, they have new tools and new communication methods that allow scientific knowl-edge to be shared instantly, and therefore acted upon by other sci-entists. It's like a vicious circle, except it's not vicious – it produces technological change as mankind has never experienced before. (We won't delve into the mis-uses of technology, which are many and varied, as that is not the focus of this book.)

You live in the most exciting of times. Never before in the history of mankind is it so easy for one individual to get his or her message out to the entire world. Think back just 100 years and you'll find only the primitive beginnings of the telephone & radio, let alone television and the internet. Only since the late 1990's - barely ten years ago - has it been possible to communicate via the Internet, and then it was only really useable for technically minded people. The average person found it too complicated to be worth the time involved to master it.

But now everything has changed, and the playing field is level. One person with a blog can influence millions, as was demonstrated in the last election. The instant transmission of ideas is a concept once thought to be impossible, but here we are. It is here.

In this chapter we'll look at several different ways you can use the power of the internet to broadcast a message about your product or service to the entire world, or as much of it as you choose. We will investigate web sites, autoresponders, blogs, podcasts and other possible ways for you to get the word out about your product or service.

Natural Search

When people who are online - who have an internet account - are interested in a given subject, they go to a "search box" on Google or MSN or Yahoo or any of a number of other portal sites and type in whatever they are looking for. Let's say you played guitar back in high school and over the years you've been busy with life and have pretty much forgotten all you knew about guitar. So you go to Google and type in "guitar lessons" or maybe "guitar tabs" or perhaps "guitar chords". In a millisecond Google returns 5,800,000 results numbered from 1 to 5,800,000. If you have the rest of your life free, you could go through all those 5,800,000 results and check them all out. But what you'll probably do is see something that interests you on the first page – the first 10 results – and you'll click on the link going to that particular web site. If you don't find what you like, you'll move down the list until you find something that does interest you.

Whatever your product or service is, as long as you have a web site, your site will come up in those "natural search" (also called "organic search") results along with all other sites in your field. But unless your site comes up on the 1 page of the search results, you don't have much of a chance for people to find you. So your job is to optimize your site so that it does come up as high as possible in the search results. Here's some basic ways to make sure it does:

The first step to marketing any page, product, or service on the Internet (as opposed to advertising in print) is to select keywords. This is because everything on the Internet responds to keywords: search engines use them to determine the topic of a site, PPC services use them to determine which ads to display, and anyone searching for a topic on the Web will enter keywords. A variety of tools are available for researching keyword popularity including the Overture® Keyword Selector tool found at www.inventory.overture.com. Type your main keyword into the search box there and a whole list of keyphrases will come up showing their relative popularity.

Buy a domain name that contains the keywords about what you do or sell. For example if you are a guitar teacher, buy a domain name such as "guitar-lessons-universe.com" or some such name.

Use your keywords early and often. If your product is guitar lessons, then make sure you use those two words in your headline and many times in the body of the site. But don't be ridiculous about it – it has to read naturally. A word density of 5% or so is usually about right. Now when the search engine spiders crawl through your site, they will "see" those words and know what your page is about and rank your page accordingly in the search results. I like to use a keyword phrase in my headline, sub-head, many times in the body copy, and again at the very bottom of the page so the search engine spiders will have no doubt what my page is about.

The phrase "guitar lessons" will have enormous competition, so you should narrow that down by creating many pages for your site, each one optimized for a different keyword phrase. For example, if you live and teach in Auburn California then make a separate page using the key phrase "guitar lessons Auburn California". If you specialize in jazz, create a separate page using the keywords "jazz guitar lessons". The more specialized you can make the keyword, the better the chance it will come up high in the search results. In my field of I have several hundred different pages, each created around a specific keyword phrase.

Use the same keyword phrases in your meta tags (the identification code behind each page – your ISP or webmaster can help you with it) and in the file name. For example, if you create a page centered around the phrase "guitar tabs for songs", name the page using that name. That will create a file name of www.guitar-lessons-universe.com/guitar-tabs-for-songs.html.

Submit your site to all the major search engines using a free submission service such as www.submitexpress.com or just by going to each individual search engine and looking for a link that says something like "Submit your site" or "Submit your URL".

Create your own blog by going to www.blogger.com It is absolutely free and very easy to set up your own blog (short for "web log" – like an online diary). Write a few paragraphs about your business and include a link to your web site. Search engines love blogs because they are nearly all text and easy to crawl, so when their spider crawls your blog it will find a link to your web site, making your web site more likely to be listed quickly. Not only that, but your blog itself might get picked up and publicized in other blogs or web sites if they find your content interesting.

Pay Per Click Ads

There is another way to get on page one of the search results, and that is to pay for it using Pay-Per-Click ads. With Pay-Per-Click (PPC) or Pay-for-Performance advertising, you only pay for advertising when an action takes place; in this case, when the user clicks the ad. This enables you to place ads right next to those of multi-million dollar corporations, except you don't have to spend a million dollars – would you believe that $5. gets you started, and then only pay when someone actually clicks on your ad? Here are a couple of the top companies where you can place your ads:

Yahoo® Search Marketing

Formerly known as Overture®, Yahoo has been in the "natural search" (non-advertising) and keyword advertising business longer than Google®. Yahoo Search Marketing offers search engine marketing, local advertising across the Web, and tools for submitting your site to search engines, Yahoo Travel, and the Yahoo directory. There are three categories to choose from:

Sponsored search:

According to Yahoo®, this service allows you to reach "up to 90%" of Internet users. These are the results you see in search engines such as Yahoo!, MSN, and AltaVista.

Content Match:

Yahoo sometimes categorizes this as part of Sponsored Search, but it is a distinct entity. With Content Match, your ads are placed beside articles within the Yahoo publisher's network. That network includes MSN, CNN, National Geographic, and many others. This is a dynamic network, so check with Yahoo to find the latest information.

Local Advertising:

With the Local advertising feature, you are able to target customers in your geographical area when they are searching Yoohoo sites. When the customer searches, your listing appears inside the "Sponsor Results" area. When customers click on the listing, they are provided with your custom "Locator Page," which contains information such as your address, business hours, map, Web site, and more.

To learn all about the services available, visit the Yahoo Search Marketing site http://searchmarketing.yahoo.com

Google Adwords®

Google Adwords provides a great opportunity for beginners to get started with online advertising. The system is straightforward, even simple enough for the absolute beginner. It is also enough to power large marketing campaigns with tracking and forecasting technologies built directly into your account. Best of all, it only costs $5 to get started.

Adwords will automatically set the price you pay to one cent above the next nearest competitor. Nobody is allowed to reserve the top position (positioning is based on ad performance and the amount you are willing to pay per click), and you can target specific countries or regions. You can target both search pages and the "Google Network," which includes the broad range of large commercial sites and the myriad blogs that carry Google Adsense® ads. To learn the fine details of the Adwords, be sure to study the Adwords Help Center at https://adwords.google.com/support).

Google® Adwords® is in many ways a simpler system than that provided by Yahoo! Search Marketing. The core offerings are listed below and described in brief.

Search Targeting:

Listings are placed on Google search results pages. While the listing displays, Google tracks the Click Through Rate (CTR – the number of clicks divided by the number of times displayed) to determine whihch ads are most successful. These are displayed more. The actual display is averaged throughout the month, day, and year, in accordance with your budget.

Contextual Targeting:

Displaying ads in the content network is optional, but especially helpful because the CTR here does not affect the CTR of your Search Pages Listings. This is a far-reaching service, touching sites that range from Amazon.com to one-person blogs. Also included are listings in the Gmail service, newsletters, and virtually any other kind of site you can imagine. The content of the page is compared to the keywords of the ad to find a good match.

Site Targeting:

Site Targeting is a feature of Google Content Network listings that allows you to stipulate which sites can display your ad, and which ones cannot. When targeting sites, you will first list the sites for inclusion. You can also simply provide a keyword list of sites that describe your site and allow the Adwords system to find matching sites on the Google Network. If you need to check whether a site does or does not display Adwords ads, the most direct approach is to visit the site for yourself, since Adwords does not serve up that information.

Local Targeting:

You can specify the exact area you want your ad to display in. This information is based on Adword's ability to determine the location of the visitor by his or her IP address; it is not foolproof, but for the most part reliable. For local targeting your options are countries and territories, regions/cities, and customized. The customized option displays ads within whatever distance you specify from your business. If you need to reach a particular group of people, local targeting is one method for doing so.

Language targeting:

There's no reason to advertise in English to your French-speaking Canadian customers, and now you don't have to. E"Ad Group" name. Immediately after setting this name, set the target language from the scroll-down box. The next step will allow you to set your country (see "Local Targeting," above).

Miva®

Once you have mastered advertising on Google Adwords and Yahoo Search Marketing, the next logical pay per click network is Miva "http:/ /www.miva.com" Miva is the collective brand that includes entities formerly known as FindWhat.com, Espotting Media, Miva Corporation, Comet Systems and B&B Advertising. The company offers its own network of sites that include Mitsui, Lycos, Verizon SuperPages, and ThomasB2B.com. Advertising is possible in the US and Europe. As an Advertiser, you are able to advertise your business across the Miva Network, often at rates that are less than the larger Yahoo! and Google networks. The main service of interest to an affiliate advertiser is Miva Pay-Per-Click. Like the other networks, the system relies on "bid for position" technology. Unlike Google Adwords, you are able to view the competing bids for your keywords at any time.

With Pay Per Click systems such as Yahoo Search Marketing and Google and Miva, you are able to set maximum bid limits, such as the maximum payout per day, maximum expenditure per day per campaign, and maximum to pay per keyword term. These maximums vary by service. In all PPC services be sure to specify how much you will pay for each click. In some services this may start at 1 cent. Others start at 5 cents per click, and others start at 15 cents per click.

Start cheap. For the absolute beginner, this is critical. It will take time to learn to write your ad and site copy well, so don't through too much money at the problem to begin with. Write your ad and keep your budget to the point where you can lose all the money and not feel the pain. If that means your limit is $1 per day for $30 total per month, so be it. When you start getting results, decide how much you can spend on advertising and still make a profit, then structure your advertising around it. Be sure to start small and put a daily limit on your spending! I have heard some horror stories about people who didn't put a limit on their spending and ended up with a bill of many thousands of dollars! No need for that at all – just be cautious and read the details of each PPC company.

Autoresponders

What's an autoresponder? If you've ever asked for information online about a product or service, or signed up for an e-list or group membership on the Internet, and received a nearly instantaneous response in your e-mail inbox, an autoresponder program was responsible for delivering the reply.

Simply put, autoresponders are e-mail programs that send out a preset message in response to every incoming e-mail received. Some autoresponders, like sign-up services for e-groups and forums, are one-shot deals: a single response for every message received. Just about every Internet-based company uses autoresponders for a variety of purposes, from automating tasks that would otherwise take up hundreds of man-hours to building lists and tracking prospective leads.

Multiple autoresponders send a series of messages to received e-mail addresses on a predetermined, timed basis. For instance, a multiple autoresponder can be used to send an instant response, then a follow-up message three days later, then another five days after that, and so on. It can be programmed to send a message a day, one per week, twice monthly, or any interval that satisfies the purpose of the message series.

Autoresponders are the most powerful Internet marketing tools available. They are easy to use, and once they're set up the entire marketing process is automated and instant. When you use autoresponders, your Internet business runs itself 24 hours a day. Launching an effective autoresponder campaign can mean the difference between a struggling business and a wildly successful one.

Just about any online business can benefit by using autoresponders. In fact, with a properly arranged campaign, your as-yet-unfounded business can be built around an autoresponder program.

All you need is a product and an effective series of autoresponder messages, and you can start carving your piece of the Internet pie.

Your autoresponder is your golden goose: the marketing tool that will sell your well-developed product far more effectively than any other form of advertising. Few sales are made by impulse buyers, particularly on the internet. But if you are able to get your message out repeatedly to people who are already interested in what you have to offer, you will see an explosive sales response.

An autoresponder is an e-mail based program that does exactly what its name suggests: sends out an automatic response when an e-mail is received. Nearly every successful online business uses autoresponders to achieve and maintain a big-time image without spending a fortune or lifting a finger. You've probably seen autoresponders at work if you've ever signed up for an e-zine, newsletter, or other electronic mailing list. The instant you send a message to the subscription address, you receive a reply with either a welcome message or a request to confirm your subscription by clicking a link. Most list-building software comes with built-in autoresponders, and many web hosts are now offering autoresponder options for the custom e-mail addresses they come with.

When you set up an autoresponder, you don't have to make delivery instantaneous. Autoresponders allow you to pv reset a series of messages to be delivered on a timed basis to each address it receives: you can send out several messages once a day, every other day, once a week, or even once a month. This makes autoresponders great tools for marketing and newsletter delivery.

Newsletters and e-zines

Using autoresponders is a great way to manage subscription lists for newsletter and e-zines. You can keep all your contact e-mail addresses in one place, allowing you to send your newsletter as well as occasional updates and special offers. If you write your newsletters ahead of time, you can simply plug them in to an autoresponder, set the delivery date, and forget about it so you can concentrate on other things.

Viral marketing

With any message you send out from your autoresponder, you can include an incentive for people to spread the word about your product or service. You can offer a free gift, such as an exclusive e-course or a sample of your product or service, for anyone who passes along your sales letter, newsletter issue or article to a certain number of friends, usually ten or more. Viral marketing can be a rapid and powerful tool for expanding your business across the internet.

Product delivery

If your product is in an electronic format, such as an e-book or audio file, you can set an autoresponder to deliver the product instantly upon receipt of payment. This saves you a lot of time in fulfilling orders and ensures every product is delivered promptly.

Order confirmation and follow-up

Even for physical products or services, you can use an autoresponder to instantly confirm to a customer that their order has been received and will be acted upon. For order confirmation, you can set up a two-message delivery: instant confirmation, and a follow-up thank you message timed for arrival a few days after you anticipate order fulfillment. Following up with customers is a great way to ensure repeat business and project a big image.

Here are a few autoresponder companies:

- *http://www.ProAutoResponder.com*
- *http://www.aweber.com*
- *http://www.getresponse.com*
- *http://www.1shoppingcart.com*

Blogs - What the Heck is a Blog, And Why Should I Get One?

Blogs have enjoyed an explosion in popularity in the internet community. Short for web log, a blog is an online journal set in an archived format that allows for frequent updates. People use blogs for a variety of reasons, both business and personal. The popularity of blogs is so widespread that a new term has been coined to describe the massive collection of blogs existing online: the blogosphere.

There are a variety of good reasons to host a blog for your company. One is fresh content. By adding a new blog entry daily, or even weekly, you are constantly bringing new content to your site, which helps increase your search engine rankings. Another is to showcase your experience. You can create blog entries about projects you've done for clients, or share stories sent in by customers who have purchased your products. Furthermore, a blog provides another way to keep visitors interested by offering them information or entertainment—and keep them coming back for more.

Still another advantage to creating and maintaining a blog is customer interaction. A standard blog feature allows viewers to post comments and feedback on individual entries. You can set your blog to allow comments from anyone, even anonymous visitors (however, if your blog provides a word verification feature, you should turn it on to avoid spam comments...oh yes, spam is everywhere).

The blog format you choose will vary according to the type of business you run. If you run a consultation practice, make note of your clients' successes as they occur (be sure to get the client's permission before you write about them!). If you are selling a product, you can use a blog to keep consumers updated about company and industry developments. You can also transform a blog into an online resource center for information relating to your product or services. Find a few interesting links every day to related web sites and give visitors something new to look forward to every time they visit your site.

How do you get a blog? You can either maintain a separate blog from your web site, or use a web host that integrates blogging software with their packages. If you set up a separate blog, be sure to link to it from every page of your web site, and link back to your web site from your blog. Most blog hosting companies provide blog accounts free of charge. The most popular blog provider is Blogger.com (powered by search engine giant Google), followed closely by LiveJournal.com. Blog hosts generally provide customizable templates in a wide variety of styles, so you can find one that matches your web site.

Podcasting

Podcasting is a relatively new kind of technology that consists of making audio files (most commonly in MP3 format) available online in a way that allows software to automatically download the files for listening at the user's convenience – another words, timeshifting – making the audio file come to you on your terms of time and place, instead of you going to it on it's terms. The word itself, which was selected as the most important new word in 2005, comes from a combination of the Apple iPod and broadcast; hence, podcast.

Podcasting is just like having your own radio station, programmed with your favorite items and ready for you to listen anywhere, anytime. With podcasting, you can listen to whatever you want wherever you want whenever you want.

So what exactly is podcasting? A podcast is an audio file stored on the Internet that you can download to your computer or MP3 player and listen to whenever you want. Once you have produced a podcast you can allow people to subscribe to receive updates when they are uploaded to your website so they can download the podcast to their iPod or elsewhere.

There are basically three steps to publishing a podcast:

1) *Create an MP3 file of the podcast. You can find services on the web such as FeedForAll which will do this for you. Just type in "create an MP3" in Google or your favorite search engine, and you will find many firms that can help you.*

2) *Host the MP3 file on your website or another website that caters to podcasts. You might want to make a separate page telling about your podcast and showing people how to access it.*

3) *Make an RSS feed. An RSS feed is a syndication service that allows people to find your podcast and subscribe your podcast. Blogger.com will make an RSS feed for your blog, so you could use that to "feed" your podcast to subscribers.*

For the complete scoop on podcasting check out www.podcastsecretsrevealed.com

Chapter 9

How To Get an Army of Freelance Specialists All Over The World To Work For You!

Did you know that there are literally thousands of skilled people in most every field, anxious to work for you on a free-lance basis? That means you don't pay them a salary or have the problems intrinsic to hiring people, but instead they work for you on a piece basis.

For example, let's say you have a home business in a specialized field such as scrap booking or golf or wedding invitations or whatever, and you need a booklet written to describe some aspect of your product or service. You can go to a site such as www.elance.com and at no cost to you list your project on their site, and writers from around the world will see your ad and bid on your job. In my experience you will get anywhere from 5 to 25 bids, and then you can look at their past work that they have done for others, check the rating that others have given them, and ask them questions until you have found the person that you think can do the job.

The problem usually is that there are so many good writers to choose from that it's difficult to narrow down the field. But that's a bonus for you, as you can take your time and select from the best. Once you have found a writer you really like, you can turn to them again and again for other projects that you might need.

The same is true of software, music, animation, web creation, sales material, multi-media, and on and on. There's hardly a field where you couldn't find a number of qualified people to help you, and the cost is often much less than you would pay if you just ran an ad in your local newspaper. That's because in many other countries the wage-scale is much lower than in the US, and skilled people in India and China and many other countries are anxious to find freelance work in the US.

There are many advantages to using freelance contractors rather than hiring permanent employees. There is less paperwork involved, and you don't have to pay Social Security, Medicare or unemployment taxes for contractors. Additionally, nearly every industry has a pool of freelancers who specialize in performing the services you need. As long as you are careful in hiring a freelance, their services can be extremely helpful in keeping your home business running smoothly.

Freelancers are available for just about any aspect of your business you can imagine. There are freelance writers who specialize in web copy; graphic designers to create and maintain web sites; jingle songwriters to create ads; software programmers who will create custom software for you to use or sell; companies that create and launch advertising campaigns; general and market research specialists; optimization and search engine submission companies; toll-free call center services...the list is endless. When you decide which area you need help in, you can then look for a contractor whose area of expertise matches your needs.

Many freelance contractors advertise their availability on job boards and classified sites. Most have a web site where you can view samples of their work or find out who some of their previous clients have been. There is usually no need to pay more than the competitive rate; and those who undercharge might offer a lower quality service. However, their work samples may prove otherwise, and in any case you should go with a contractor who will give you what you're looking for.

Often it is to your benefit to let freelancers come to you rather than seek one out yourself. It is far easier and makes for a better working relationship to sort through qualified candidates who are already interested in the job you're offering. Placing an effective job advertisement will bring you plenty of contractors to choose from.

Whenever you deal with a freelancer, it is important to have a contract for their services. This can be a simple document that states what work the contractor has agreed to do, how much you are paying them for it, when the work will be completed, and how the finished project will be delivered. A verbal agreement is not enough to protect you if something goes wrong and the freelancer is unable to deliver a completed project, so be sure and get a signed agreement or contact.

If you're wearing all the business hats yourself, accomplishing the many tasks associated with running a home business can become confusing. One technique that can help you keep your life organized is to set aside blocks of your business day and use that time to deal with specific functions. For example, you can spend the first hour answering customer correspondence; the next few fulfilling orders; the next couple in planning marketing strategies, writing ads; then the next segment of time taking care of your bookwork. Schedule separate times to update your web site, deal with suppliers and creditors, and manage your business advertising. It's easier to manage multiple departments if you know what type of tasks you'll be handling ahead of times. You can even give yourself different titles for each portion of your workday — I'm known variously as "the garbage man", "the cat feeder", and several other titles in addition to "musician", "instructor", "webmaster", and so on. One of the great things about a home business is the constant variety. When you wear all the hats, there's never a dull moment!

At some point in the formation and development of your home business, you will probably need help in some area of your life. There are many people who work for another company out of their own home and communicate with their employers via e-mail and telephone. In fact most freelancers and contractors work in this manner all the time. Some companies hire "permanent" freelancers – that is, they use the same people over and over. By enlisting free-lancers rather than having employees "come" to work, you save on the expenses of providing additional equipment and furnishings—as well as the potential problems that may result from people coming to your home to work.

Freelancers, or virtual assistants as they are sometimes known, are a fast-growing sector of the business industry. Many people are choosing to work from home, and making their services available to other companies rather than starting their own businesses. Good freelancers often come pre-packaged with their own equipment, software, phone lines—everything you have in your home office, and sometimes more. There are thousands of people like this available to help your business, either as permanent employees or freelance contractors.

There are a huge number of web sites dedicated to telecommuting and working from home concerns, including job boards, classified ad sites and professional listings of established telecommuters. These boards generally work two ways: you can search them for talent, or post a job advertisement and have the talent come to you.

If you need part-time or full-time help on a permanent basis, you might want to consider hiring a virtual employee or two. There are several ways to regulate and manage virtual employees. You can assign them to "work" at specified times, for instance, if you needed someone to answer phones during peak business hours. There are many virtual administrative assistants trained to perform routine office tasks from a remote location. Just as a typical business secretary would do from the front desk of a brick-and-mortar office, a virtual administrative assistant can answer phones and e-mails, fulfill orders, manage lists and databases, and take care of other time-consuming tasks; leaving you free to run your home business and do what you do best.

You can also hire a freelancer on a piecework basis, of course. If your business involves generating projects on an individual basis for clients, such as consultation work, you could hire a part-time virtual employee to work on your overflow and pay them on a per-project basis, rather than an hourly rate.

One benefit of hiring a freelancer is the ability to develop their skills in relation to your home business. Because employees involve a longer time frame and level of commitment than contractors, you can develop a relationship with your employees and eventually, they will be able to manage themselves with little supervision. Be sure to invest enough time and energy in your freelance employees to keep them happy working for you, and your job will be far easier in the long run.

Most home businesses choose to work with freelance contractors rather than hire permanent employees. There is less paperwork involved, and you don't have to pay Social Security, Medicare or unemployment taxes for contractors. Additionally, nearly every industry has a pool of freelancers who specialize in performing the services you need. As long as you are careful in hiring a contractor, their services can be extremely helpful in keeping your home business running smoothly.

Here are some web sites where you can find good free-lance people to do most anything you need, from writing to web design to software creation:

- www.Elance.com
- www.IFreelance.com
- www.Freelancewriting.com
- www.GetaCoder.com
- www.workaholics4hire.com

- www.scriptlance.com
- www.sologig.com
- www.Rent-a-Coder.com
- www.CodeLance.com

Like traditional employees, freelancers and contractors must be paid. You can opt to mail a paper check to them, but this is often just one more hassle in an already complicated home office setup. It also costs extra money in printing and mailing costs.

One way that is growing in popularity is to pay freelancers through the internet. Monetary transactions online are much safer than they used to be, and there are several large companies who deal specifically with electronic funds transfers. The most popular of these is PayPal, which allows any two individuals with PayPal accounts (which are free, by the way - there's no charge for signing up) to exchange money online. You can register checking accounts, savings accounts, and even credit cards with PayPal, and most virtual telecommuters and freelancers already have PayPal accounts. Paying them is a simple matter of signing in to your account and allocating funds from your checking account—and PayPal takes care of the rest.

You can also set up online transfers between checking accounts, or direct deposit for permanent employees. Most banks will allow you to do this right from their web site, without ever setting foot in a branch office.

Hiring a freelancer or contractor is a great way to expand your home business, and the process will help you learn more about online business. A good freelancer can be invaluable in making your home business develop faster, and you won't have to spend a fortune in the process. I have used freelancers for writing articles, composing, writing e-books, developing software, web site redesign, and more. I think you will be delighted with how much work you can get done at home "with a little help from your (freelance) friends."

Chapter 10

How To Run Your Home Business With a Minimum of Headaches and Make It a Joy to Operate

Early in your home business career, you'll have to make a decision. At some point you will be tempted, if your business is thriving, to hire employees, rent or build a building, in other words, aim toward building an empire. So you'll need to ask yourself "should I remain as free as possible, and limit my growth or farm out most of my work?"

That question may not seem particularly germane at this point in your business, but sooner or later you'll have to face it.

If you choose the former path – that of "empire building", there is plenty of material – books, college courses, etc. – to help you on your way. I won't say anything about that path, because I don't know much about it, and because of my personality and life-style, I really don't care to. But I wish you well. One of my good friends, Craig Black, has taken a little home business and turned it into a good-sized business with about 100 employees and a big building with no end in sight.

But for me that sounds exactly like what I don't want – I want to be free to come to work in my tennis shoes and choose my working hours and so on. Does that sound like a cop-out? So be it. I love my life-style, and I wouldn't trade it for a big corporate identity for anything. I earn a very satisfactory living, and yet I have no employees, no time clock, no rigid schedule, no large investment in buildings, equipment, etc. like you normally associate with an entrepreneur.

A Family Lifestyle

Here's what I wrote about this lifestyle years ago when the kids were small – and it's still true today:

"As I write these words, I am sitting in the corner chair of our cabin at Diamond Lake in the Cascade mountains of Oregon, fireplace roaring, kids playing Monopoly on the rug, Bev in the kitchen frying the trout we caught last night. Instead of a suit and tie, I'm wearing my comfortable old clothes and tennis shoes. In a minute my wife will get after me to go cut that wood I've been promising to cut all day, but first I'm going to finish writing this page. Besides, the chain saw needs oil, and I can't use it until I drive to the South Shore store to buy some, so I might as well wait until tomorrow now. We'll go out trolling again after dinner, then over to the lodge for a late snack.

Sound good? It is good. We travel whenever the work is caught up, and I write as we travel. (I've written 53 pages while here at the lake the past three days. That will pay for this trip and probably 20 other trips.) When we get home, we'll play tennis (we have our own court), spend time with the kids (we read together as a family all the time – things like "The Chronicles of Narnia" by C , S, Lewis, "Pilgrims Progress" by Bunyan – that sort of thing) and when the kids are in bed, Bev and I will go out to our little music studio (a separate building 30 ft. from our house) and catch up on our work. While we were gone, we had half -a-dozen people working for us on a freelance basis – no hours to keep -strictly on a piece basis – order processors, mailing people, layout artists, and if you want to count all the people selling for us on an affiliate basis, hundreds of others as well.

All this isn't to say we don't work hard – we sure do – but we pick our hours and we work together, sometimes as a family, always Bev and I. Its kind of funny, too, that money has never been our ultimate goal. Our goal has been to create worthwhile products that help people learn, sell them at a reasonable price, and spend a maximum amount of time with our family. Yet the money has come along as a kind of by-product, and we're thankful for it. But it would not severely disrupt our lives if we did not have money, since it is only a means to a goal, not a goal in itself."

Do I have your mouth watering yet? If this sort of lifestyle appeals to you – if you are a family man rather than a corporate executive – then take a look at some of the methods I've found which make all this possible:

Farm out everything you can't do yourself. Don't hire an assistant – you'll have to withhold taxes, buy insurance, keep time, worry about working conditions, conform to 47 government agency regulations, etc. Don't buy a printing press. Your printer can do a far better job than you can, and besides, when you own a press you need a camera, then a folder, then a paper cutter, then a typesetting machine, etc., etc. You'll be way ahead to let a printer do all that for you.

"Hire" a neighbor lady on your block to help you with your typing, mailings, addressing, and so on. She can work at home on a piece basis – 2 cents per envelope addressed, or whatever is fair.

"Hire" a local artist to do your layout and design work on his own time at his own place.

"Hire" an advertising agency to place your ads for you. It doesn't cost any more than if you placed the ads yourself, and it saves countless hours of correspondence, bill paying, and so forth. The agency gets its payment from the magazines and newspapers – 15% of your ad cost. So in essence, you get the services of an advertising agency at no cost to you. "Hire" a printer to not only do your printing, but to supply you with ideas on what can be done, how to do it better, and so forth. Rely heavily on the expertise of your suppliers. They have spent years developing their knowledge in that area, and you can draw upon it at no cost to you as long as you are an active customer!

Once your list of inquiries and/or customers grows to 25,000 or more names, "hire" a computer house or list management house to handle and maintain your list. They can do in minutes what it would take you days to do; things like checking your list for duplicates, sorting it into zip code sequence so you can mail under the bulk mail rate, addressing your envelopes – and if they have a letter shop like many computer houses do, they can insert, seal, address, sort into zip code sequence, bag, and mail your entire mailing without you ever seeing it! And for less than you could do it by hand. not to mention the hours involved.

"Hire" a local CPA to set up your books for you, show you how to keep adequate records, and compute your taxes. He'll save you both money and headaches – and future problems with the IRS. Have him set up an retirement program for you so that you can contribute up to 15% of your net income to your own retirement program, and get a 100% tax deduction on it.

"Hire" as many of these "free lance employees" as you can – every one of them is an asset to you, instead of a liability. You'll find that you can do a gross business of six figures per year without a single regular employee -something not one business in a thousand can do. As a matter of fact, with the continued sophistication of the computer and the world-wide web, I believe it is theoretically possible for one individual to do a gross business of up to a million dollars per year all by himself – with a little help from his free-lance friends!

Build a family of related products. Why? Because that way you can sell to your customers over and over again. Let's say you are knowl-edgeable about old bottles and you created an e-book about collect-ing old bottles. If the people you sold the e-book to were interested in your book about bottle collecting, they'll also be interested in your next book titled The Bottle Book; An Illustrated History Of The Bottle. Then when you publish The Bottle Collectors Newsletter, they will be prime prospects. To say nothing of their interest in your Slide Chart Of Old Bottle Values, or your Directory Of Sources For Old Bottles. See how it works? You don't have to go out and hustle new customers every time you bring out a new product – you can offer the new item to your growing list of old customers.

Our first product was a music book titled How To Read Music In One Evening. Our next product was a book titled Seven Magic Steps To Speed Sight Reading, which went on where the first book left off. Did I sell that second book to many of my original customers'? You bet I did – over 50% of them. Then came How To Play Chord Piano In Ten Days! followed by How To Dress Up Naked Music On The Piano followed by Praise & Gospel Piano followed by Piano Runs & Fills and on and on. And every new title after that was offered to those same customers, and many of them purchased one or more of the new products. Then we came up with the idea of putting the content of the music books on cassette tape, so I would sit at my piano and teach through the book so that students could not only see the book, but they could also hear me explain it with musical examples I would record as I talked. So naturally we offered the cassette to people who already owned the book, as well as offering it to new people as a combo – the book and the cassette tape packaged together.

Later when videos became mainstream we took the same book and shot a video of me at the piano playing and explaining what was in each book. So then we packaged the book, cassette, and video together and offered it to our customers as well as to new people.

Then when CD's and DVD's started taking the place of cassettes and videos we switched to that format, again offering them to both existing customers and new prospects.

Now when I come out with a new product, I have a customer list of many thousands to which I can mail – either regular mail or e-mail – and if my offer is good, I'll sell hundreds or thousands of units of my new product without ever having to advertise for new customers. That is like money in the bank as long as your product line is growing. And of course I'm getting new customers and prospects every day.

But if your product line is not consistent – if you have a book on fishing and a sewing kit – you won't sell to your own customers nearly as much. There are exceptions to this rule, but for the most part, stick with a family of products, and you'll find yourself selling and re-selling the same old satisfied customers.

Locate other products related to your product to sell to your customers. This is the same principle as building a family of products. Search for other products that are compatible with your products, and offer them to your customers either by mail or by e-mail or both. You don't necessarily have to spend much money to do it, either. Arrange with the supplier to have him drop-ship for you, like you drop-ship for your dealers. Or, if it is a digital product such as an e-book, it can be delivered digitally just through a simple download. This way you don't have to lay out any cash in advance. If it is a product you will market by mail, just prepare a circular on the product, mail it to your customer list along with your own offers and when orders come in, keep your commission and forward the order to the supplier for him to drop-ship under your label. If it is a digital product, just e-mail your customers telling them about how you like the product and directing them to the site the product is on, keyed with your affiliate code so you get the credit for the sale. (For complete information on the affiliate process, see the chapter on "How to Work at Home Even If You Don't Have a Product or Service of Your Own.")

We do this. In addition to our own products, which we have developed, we have located several other musical items, which we promote on an affiliate basis. It is very profitable as long as it is in the same product line, and as long as you have a customer list to which you can mail or e-mail.

Make your customer list your most valuable asset, we mentioned above why your list is your most valuable asset. Treat it as such. Don't offer shabby products to your customers. Don't rent your list to other firms without the permission of your customers. I know it is done all the time, and you may choose to do it too, since you can earn some good additional money doing it, but my advise is to not do it. I have never rented our customer list to anyone, and never intend to. I believe it weakens the quality of the list, and tends to spoil the relationship you build up over the years with many customers. If you choose to disagree, fine, but at least make sure of the integrity of the firm renting your list. You owe your customers that much.

Now a prospect list is a different can of worms. We have an inquiry file of people who have inquired about our products, but who have never ordered. I have no particular responsibility to that list, and feel justified in renting it out occasionally. But once that prospect becomes a customer, the relationship changes. I have accepted his money, and he deserves my confidentiality. So I give it to him.

If you have a customer list of say, 1000, and you can re-sell 25% of that list yearly at an average order of $100., that means that list is worth $2500. per year to you, when your list grows to 10,000 names, it is worth $25000. per year (ignoring attrition and new customers).

When it gets to 100,000 names, your list is worth $250,000. per year to you. Of course lists vary greatly in their value depending upon the product line, and some will not be this valuable and some will be much more valuable. But the point is if you foster a specialized family of products to offer to your list, and make new offers regularly in a variety of promotional formats, your list could very well be worth more than the example above.

Back when we started maintaining our customer list we had "Addressette" master cards. They were like IBM cards in which there is a die-cut hole filled in with a stencil. By typing through a carbon tab onto the stencil, the customers name and address was available for instant addressing. Then we spread a duplicating fluid over a small area on the face of an envelope, placed the card over that space, and ran over it with a rubber roller. There was room on the card for you to pencil in a record of your customers orders – how much, what for, when shipped, and so on. The cards then were filed in alphabetical order, or by state, or whatever method we chose. That sounds so primitive now with the advent of the personal computer and databases such as FileMaker pro, but for the time it worked just fine.

Now you'll want to maintain your list on a database such as File-Maker Pro or Microsoft Access or some similar system. It's not the system you use that is important – it's maintaining your list of customers and prospects, as they are your most valuable assets.

Never handle a piece of correspondence twice. I got this principle from Joe Cossman (along with many other principles and I heartily concur. When you open your mail, act on each piece of mail immediately. Either answer it, order it, file it, or throw it away. This will cut down on your workload to an amazing degree, and keep your desk uncluttered.

Set Goals for Your Family & Your Business

Set goals for yourself your business and your family. Determine first your long-range goals by writing them own in a "Goals" notebook. Then write down how you intend to reach that goal, what short-range goals are necessary to reach your long-range goals? Then set daily goals. What are the five most important things I must accomplish today? Start to work on the most important of the five, and then if I only manage to get to number three, at least I will have done the three most important.

Goals form an extremely important part of my life. Several times a month my wife Bev and I get together to evaluate progress toward our various goals and set new goals in the area of our business and our personal lives.

Set some goals for yourself and then work for their attainment. The reason most people never get anywhere is because they don't have a clear idea of where they want to go. If you don't know where you're going, there's not much chance you're going to get there!

Borrow heavily from the genius and experience of other people. How? Through books, courses, seminars, newsletters – any fountain of knowledge that advances your present knowledge. I know it sounds like a truism but do you realize what a rare privilege it is to have free public libraries with thousands of books containing thousands of facts and insights that took accumulated lifetimes to learn? Wow! What a goldmine. But like so many things that are free and easily accessible, we take it for granted, and don't mine the riches there.

Without even considering the intellectual value of reading, your library is still a goldmine of business facts and ideas. Go look at all the directories in your library – there are markets galore for your product in those directories, if only you'll take the time to learn how to use them. Yellow pages from all the major cities provide both suppliers and accurate market lists for you. Specialized periodicals will tell you about new developments in your field, giving you ideas for new products. The vertical file houses a vast wealth of pamphlets, brochures, and clippings about every subject from angels to zebras.

Enough said, I probably won't sell you on the idea if you're not sold by now, (And did you know that your librarian will do much of your research for you if you tell her or him what you're after?)

I got my start when I read about a guy named Joseph Cossman who had made over a million dollars in mail order (that was a huge amount back in the 60's!). He was holding a one-day seminar at the Biltmore Hotel in downtown Los Angeles teaching people his techniques. The seminar cost $99. which at the time was as big as the national debt relative to my income. But somehow we got the money together and I took the Greyhound Bus from Sacramento where I lived at the time to Los Angeles, traveling all night and arriving at 7 in the morning. To say that I felt out of place walking into the Biltmore in my windbreaker among all the suits would be an understatement. But as soon as the seminar started at 9AM I knew I had come to the right place. Joe showed how he had found products to market, how he had sold them to mail order catalogs by the thousands, how he had gotten free news releases on his products, and lots more.

I was so excited at the end of the day that I spent the overnight ride home in the Greyhound scribbling madly in my notebook and making plans galore for the days to come. It turned out to be the best investment of my life (my business life – not counting my personal life) as that $99 gradually turned into hundreds and then thousands and then hundreds of thousands and a lifetime of happiness doing what I love most and working out of my own home.

Devise an answer sheet to answer common questions that are asked repeatedly about your product. Print it and include it in all your correspondence. Post it on your web site under Q&A. It will save you hours of time repeatedly answering the same questions. (This is another idea which I owe to Joe Cossman.)

Don't borrow money until your product is selling well. Many beginners think that only if they bad several thousand dollars to promote their product, they would have it made. Nothing could be further from the truth. To borrow money on an unproven product is to consign your future to continual debt. You will learn far more if you have to scrape your pennies together to print that first news release than if you had a thousand dollars to spend on it. After your product is being marketed successfully, then use the bank's money to expand. But not before. It's just too dangerous.

Price your product so everybody profits. Your goal in product pricing should be to sell your product at as low a price as possible, allowing both you and your various distributors to make a good profit. Does that sound contradictory? It shouldn't, After all, you are in business to make money, and nobody benefits if you don't make a profit. Whenever small business profits decline, the whole economy declines. The best thing you can do for your country's economy is to make an honest profit.

On the other hand, you want your product as widely distributed as possible, and the lower the price (generally), the greater the distribution you will achieve. So you want to hit a happy medium.

Price your product reasonably, but don't try to operate on too narrow a margin, or you'll find yourself working for nothing. And that won't do anybody any good.

Get local publicity for your product. If you desire to do so, you can obtain a substantial amount of local publicity by the following means:

Present copies of your book, song, or service to local opinion makers, such as your mayor, the head of your school board, your librarian, police chief, or whoever would be the appropriate person to receive your product.

Call up your local newspaper and tell them what you're doing. Often the "local girl/boy makes good" aspect will bring a news story. I have gotten at least a dozen write-ups in my local paper, and my neighbor Norm Bruce got a nice write-up just the other day in our local paper, including a photo of his Granada Pitching Machine in action. Your newspaper is looking for news -provide them with some about you and your product,

Call up your local radio and TV stations and ask them if you can appear on their "talk" shows with your new product. Chances are they will be glad for the opportunity to have a local author or inventor on their show.

Let your friends know what you're doing, (But don't brag!) Spread the word about your product. You never know what chain of events might begin from a chance exposure. I have located new markets this way, and I have located new products to sell this way.

Chapter 10: Making Your Business a Joy to Operate

Bonus Chapter

Learn how to get your free 52 week subscription to "Secrets You Absolutely, Positively Need To Know To Turn Your Home Business Into a Raging Success!"

Working at home has been such a tremendous blessing in my life that I want to share some of the insights and experiences that flow from having a business at home.

And since this is a "skinny book", there are many more things I would love to share with you – things like:

- The best home office equipment and furniture to get
- How to use your telephone answering machine as a sales vehicle
- How to make your home business safe from intruders
- How to get a merchant account
- How to make your sales materials "viral" so your message will spread quickly
- Ways to let your family members participate in your home business and at the same time strengthen your family life
- Ways to maximize the tax advantages of a home business
- How to sell stuff you don't own to people you never see (legally!)
- How to use video on your web site to promote your business
- How to use the power of sequential emails
- Directories that will list your business free of charge
- Software that broadcasts articles & news releases all over the web
- How to set up an online affiliate program so other people can

sell your products
- *How to get your podcasts on eTunes and other sites*
- *How to use Google Video to promote your business at no cost*

Since we're out of space in this little book, I am going to give you a bonus - a free 1-year subscription to my e-mail newsletter titled "Secrets You Absolutely, Positively Need To Know To Turn Your Home Business Into a Raging Success!" Just go to a special page that I have set up just for readers of this book and enter your name and email address. Your free subscription will start immediately.

Here's the web address:

http://www.home-business-music.com/bonus.htm

www.ingramcontent.com/pod-product-compliance
Lightning Source LLC
Jackson TN
JSHW080853211224
75817JS00002B/25